Birds in Mind
Australian Nature Poems

Andrew Lansdown

Wombat Books

Birds in Mind

Published by Wombat Books
P. O. Box 1519, Capalaba Qld 4157, Australia
www.wombatbooks.com.au

978-1-921633-04-1

Copyright © Andrew Lansdown, 2009
www.andrewlansdown.com

Cover Illustration: Little Kingfisher, 1995
Gouache on Arches paper, 20 x 30 cm, by Peter Good
Photo of cover painting: Dwight Randall

Back cover illustration: Andrew Lansdown, 1981
Acrilic on board, 60 x 45 cm, by Peter Good

Design and layout: Rochelle Manners

National Library of Australia Cataloguing-in-Publication entry

Author:	Lansdown, Andrew Trevor, 1954-
Title:	Birds in mind : Australian nature poems / Andrew Lansdown.
ISBN:	9781921633041 (pbk.)
Subjects:	Nature--Poetry.
Dewey Number:	A823.1

Even the sparrow finds a home,
and the swallow a nest for herself,
where she may lay her young,
at your altars, O LORD of hosts,
my King and my God.
The Sons of Korah, The Holy Bible, Psalm 84:3

Look at the birds of the air: they neither sow nor reap nor gather
into barns, and yet your heavenly Father feeds them.
Jesus, The Holy Bible, Matthew 6:26

Andrew Lansdown was born in 1954 in Pingelly, Western Australia, and currently lives with his family in Perth, where he works as a writer, editor and lecturer. He studied at Curtin University of Technology, Murdoch University and Edith Cowan University, and has worked as a public servant clerk, a garage attendant, a TAFE tutor, a prison education officer, a church pastor, and country newspaper journalist. He is the author of nine books of poetry and five books of fiction. His poetry has been widely published in magazines, newspapers and anthologies. He has won the Western Australian Premier's Prize for Poetry (twice) and the Adelaide Festival's John Bray National Poetry Award.

Highly respected for his poems dealing with family, faith and the human condition, Lansdown is also acclaimed for his imagist and nature poetry. In *A Reader's Guide to Contemporary Australian Poetry* (UQP, 1995), Geoff Page states: 'Lansdown is able to suggest very deftly and concisely the so-called "thisness" of things, especially things in nature, for example plants and birds … [He] is one of the most assured of Australian poets working in the Imagist tradition … he has written a considerable number of poems which are perfect examples of their kind. They have a descriptive exactness and a seeming spontaneity, combining to produce a text to which one can imagine no change being made without damage.'

Also by Andrew Lansdown

Poetry
Homecoming
Counterpoise
Windfalls
Waking and Always
The Grasshopper Heart
Between Glances
Fontanelle

Children's Poetry
A Ball of Gold

Short Stories
The Bowgada Birds
The Dispossessed

Poems, Stories, Essays
Abiding Things

Novels
With My Knife (USA edition, *Beyond the Open Door*)
Dragonfox
The Red Dragon

Acknowledgements

Many poems in this collection have been published in the following magazines and newspapers: *The Adelaide Review; The Age; Alive Magazine; Amity; Antipodes* (USA); *Artlook; Aquarius* (UK); *The Asahi Shimbun* (Japan); *Blue Dog; The Briefing; The Bulletin; The Canberra Times; Chronicles* (USA); *Christians Writing; Fremantle Arts Review; Helix; The Heron's Nest* (USA); *The Horatian; Identity; Imago; Island; Linq; Lynx: A Journal of Linking Poets* (USA); *Marginata; Meanjin; Micropress Yates; Northern Perspective; On Being; Overland; OzMuze; Paper Wasp; Patterns; Poetry Australia; Poetry Kanto* (Japan); *Quadrant; Quark: Young People's Magazine; Salt; Southerly; Southern Review; Studio; This Australia; Verse* (Scotland); *The Weekend Australian; The West Australian; Westerly; The Western Mail; The Western Review; The Western Word; Writing Australia.*

Some poems in this collection have also been published in the following anthologies: (1) *Poet's Choice: An Anthology of New Australian Poetry*, ed, Philip Roberts (Bundeena: Island Press, 1977). (2) *Poet's Choice: An Anthology of New Australian Poetry*, ed, Philip Roberts (Bundeena: Island Press, 1978). (3) *Poet's Choice: An Anthology of New Australian Poetry*, ed Philip Roberts (Bundeena: Island Press, 1979). (4) *Summerland: A Western Australian Sesquicentenary Anthology of Poetry and Prose*, eds, Alec Choate & Barbara York Main (University of Western Australia Press, 1979). (5) *Quarry: a selection of contemporary western australian poetry*, ed, Fay Zwicky (Fremantle Arts Centre Press, 1981). (6) *Poems On My Mind*, ed, Anne Gunter, (Melbourne: Longman Cheshire, 1981). (7) *Lines From The Horizon and other poems*, ed, Christopher Pollnitz (Mattara anthology; University of Newcastle, 1982). (8) *An Anthology of Christian Verse*, ed, Francis Byrne (Adelaide: Rigby, 1983). (9) *Poem of Thanksgiving and other poems*, ed, Paul Kavanagh (Mattara anthology; University of Newcastle, 1985). (10) *Inside Poetry*, ed, Sybille Smith (South Melbourne: Pitman, 1985). (11) *The New Oxford Book of Australian Verse*, ed, Les A. Murray (Melbourne: Oxford University Press, 1986). (12) *An Inflection of Silence and other poems*, ed, Christopher Pollnitz (Mattara anthology; University of Newcastle, 1986). (13) *Australian Poetry 1986*, ed, Vivian Smith (Sydney: Angus & Robertson, 1986). (14) *This Australia: Special Schools Edition*, ed, Lesley Howard Murdoch (Richmond: Greenhouse Publications, 1987). (15) *Properties of the Poet*, ed, Paul Kavanagh (Mattara anthology; University of Newcastle, 1987). (16) *Wordhord: A Critical Selection of Contemporary Western Australian Poetry*, ed, Dennis Haskell & Hilary Fraser (Fremantle Arts Centre Press, 1989). (17) *Zbornik Avstralskih Slovencev - 1988: Anthology of Australian Slovenes – 1988*, ed, Jose Preseren et al (Sydney: Slovenian-Australian Literary & Art Circle, 1988). (18) *Margins: A West Coast Selection of Poetry, 1829-1988*, ed, William Grono (Fremantle Arts Centre Press, 1988).

(19) *Pictures From An Exhibition*, ed, Paul Kavanagh (Mattara anthology; University of Newcastle, 1989). (20) *The Flight of the Emu: Contemporary Light Verse*, ed, Geoffrey Lehmann (Sydney: Angus & Robertson, 1990). (21) *The Sea's White Edge*, ed, Paul Kavanagh (Springwood: Butterfly Books, 1991). (22) *New Life Digest 1993*, ed, Bob Thomas (Blackburn: New Life Australia, 1992). (23) *Going Down South: Volume II*, ed, Catherine Chandler (Bunbury: South West Development Authority, 1993). (24) *Whispering in God's Ear: A New Collection of Poetry for Children*, ed, Alan MacDonald (Oxford: Lion Publishing, 1994). (25) *A Glossary of Literary Terms*, ed, Kerry Stewart (Perth: Bookland, 1994). (26) *Sudden Alchemy*, ed, Patricia Darby (Cottesloe: Fellowship of Australian Writers, 1998). (27) *Wide World of English 2*, ed, Helen Downey (South Melbourne: Pearson Education Australia [Longman], 2001). (28) *First Australian Haiku Anthology*, ed Janice M Bostok, John Bird and Jacqui Murray (Australian Haiku Society/Paper Wasp, 2003). (29) *Studio*, ed, Paul Grover (Albury: Studio, 2006). (30) *Second Australian Haiku Anthology*, ed, Janice M Bostok, Katherine Samuelowicz & Vanessa Proctor (Chapel Hill Qld: Paper Wasp, 2006). (31) *Australia's China*, ed, John Kinsella and Ouyang Yu. (32) *The Road South: An Anthology of Contemporary Australian Poetry*, ed, Ron Pretty (Bengal Creations, 2007). (33) *GROW: Under the Southern Cross*, eds, Anne Hamilton and Lyn Hurry (Kenmore, Qld: Writerlynks Grow, 2008). (34) *The Best Australian Poems 2008*, ed, Peter Rose (Melbourne: Black Inc, 2008). (35) *Little Book of Cats*, ed, Jo Karmel (Canberra: National Library of Australia, 2009).

Some poems in this collection have also been broadcast on the following radio stations/programs: Australian Broadcasting Corporation, *A First Hearing*; Australian Broadcasting Corporation, *The Poet's Tongue*; Australian Broadcasting Corporation, *PoeticA*; Radio 5UV (University of Adelaide), *Writers' Radio*.

Approximately half the poems in *Birds in Mind* are previously uncollected poems. The other poems (some in revised form) have been selected from Andrew's earlier poetry collections: *Homecoming* (Fremantle: Fremantle Arts Centre Press, 1979); *Counterpoise* (Sydney: Angus & Robertson Publishers, 1982); *Windfalls* (Fremantle: Fremantle Arts Centre Press, 1984); *Waking and Always* (Sydney: Angus & Robertson Publishers, 1987; reprinted by Picaro Press, Warners Bay, 2007); *The Grasshopper Heart* (Sydney: Collins/Angus & Robertson Publishers, 1991); *Between Glances* (Port Melbourne: William Heinemann Australia, 1993); *Fontanelle* (Melbourne: Five Islands Press, 2004); *Warrior Monk* (Warners Bay: Picaro Press, 2005).

The poet acknowledges with gratitude that many poems in this collection were written with the financial assistance of the Literature Board of the Australia Council.

Contents

A Remembrance of Robins

From the twig where they rested
I saw them flit away: two robins
white-capped and scarlet-breasted.

And for a moment they invested
the countryside with colour
from the twig where they rested.

No flower, no other bird contested
the bright display of these two—both
white-capped and scarlet-breasted.

Without warrant they arrested
me: plum blossoms seemed to bloom
from the twig where they rested.

And in departure they divested
the bush of brightness: bobbing away, robins
white-capped and scarlet-breasted.

Winter Wrens

i

Fine as thistledown—
the fluffed-up breast feathers of
the wrens in the cold.

ii

On the leafless vine
in the bloodless sun, wrens like
balls of cottonwool.

iii

So little, the wrens,
yet so immense, so immense
the midwinter cold!

Brimming

A cup on a cross-
beam in the carport,

a grass cup covered
with a cobweb gauze—

the nest some goodness
has filled to the brim

with wagtail hatchlings
that lift wobbling heads

above the low rim
and gape with gladness

each time their parents
return with insects,

not to mention twit-
chings and chatterings!

Wattles by Water

i

Fishing for redfin
with green rods, wattles scatter
pollard on a pool.

ii

The wattle blossom
on the slow current—comets
with tails of pollen.

iii

Riverbank wattles—
spattering the brown water
with their yellow spawn.

For the Blind

Sight is not the only sense
to make sense of wattles. Touch

is another. Feel the pods.
They are sentences in Braille,

ribbons of calligraphy
for the fingers of the blind.

Bud and Blossom

The eucalyptus bud:
a cup with a cap.

Lift the lid and
the filaments fizz.

This effervescence,
red, like sherbet.

The *Shodo* Egret

Engrossed, the egret
on the shore neglects
the glint of whitebait
in the sheet water

at its feet. It does not
note its reflection
needled like a tattoo
on the river's skin,

nor reflect that it
can lie as lightly
on air as an image
on liquid. Today,

fish are no food, light
no enlightenment,
flight no fancy. It seeks
another excellence.

In *shodo*, the Way
of Writing, the egret
pursues perfection.
Each measured footfall

is a meditation
in calligraphy.
Each delicate foot
is three *hosofude*,

slender brushes; and
each step is three
brushstrokes, converging
on a common point,

pointing to a past
step towards this step.
The white sand is rice
paper; and the bird

prints it repeatedly,
striving to perfect
its character. Egret—
master of spear,

subject of painting
and poetry—only
calligraphy is
lacking for inner

nobility. Now
it stands on one leg
as if poised, focused
for a final effort—

places with precision
its tri-tufted brush
through the still water.
Lifting up, it leaves,

as if beneath glass,
exquisitely, al-
most excellently,
its pristine figure.

Almost. Such sadness—
to know perfection, yet
never to reach it.
Croaking a regret

it flies to the sun,
the *shodo* egret.

Sacred Kingfisher

If I draw too close
it flies away. Otherwise
it appears not to
notice me at all—the small
kingfisher that comes
to my garden at nightfall
and sets me fishing
for image and metaphor.
It is a brush-stroke
of blue, framed among apples,
famed among feathers.
Still against the shifting leaves,
motionless, it dives
deep into the pools of praise
and surfaces with
itself, conveys nothing else.
It shapes the sprawling
tree by reference to itself:
a lone focal point.
Without knowledge of self, it
enacts itself precisely.

White Water

The unblemished water
at the river's bend
comes suddenly upon
a reef of rocks,
runs on ruffed with foam.

The rocks are a rookery
of shags—cormorants
preening their white bellies,
floating the feathers free.

And those two tree trunks
snagged by the far bank
are motor-powered canoes,
churning the chill water
with their rotary roots.

Kangaroos Crossing

Emerging from Boongarup Pool
the river flows through
an arbour of casuarinas
then widens to a ford
cobbled with round stones.

On the alluvial flats
beside the broad shallows
I disturbed three kangaroos
from their dozing. Startled,
they fled across the ford,

startling in turn a statue
that broke into a bird.
Now they're gone I see them
again: kangaroos bounding
through the troubled water

and a heron flying up.

Kangaroo Haiku

i

Out in the scrub
rising up then sinking down
kangaroo heads.

ii

First rain ... an odour
of kangaroos in the hollow
between the grasstrees.

iii

Slightly more solid
than the twilight—kangaroos
crossing the firebreak.

iv

The kangaroos—
gathering in the paddock
with the darkness.

Windmill

The windmill is a dandelion
on a tall stem. Behold, above
the yellow-petalled paddock,
an inflorescence of iron.

The stalk is a latticework,
a high scaffolding,
upholding the enormous bloom.
Dusky wood swallows lurk

along the laterals, face
each other in their Zorro masks.
A wagtail swings like a vane.
The wind gathers pace.

A sheoak by the dam
shifts in her skirts,
curtsies to the drifting duck,
the drinking lamb.

The metal corolla begins to hum.
It whirrs and whirls
as if flicked from its stem
by an invisible thumb.

Light Rain

i

If not the light rain
then the little mouthing fish—
rings on the water.

ii

A sandpapering
of rain ... then the pool's surface
is smooth once again.

iii

Mist in the valley,
smoke in the hill-heights ... rain, light
rain, falling, falling.

The Mantle of the Lamp

The moon is a mantle,
the merest tracery of white,
in the glass of the afternoon sky.

Towards evening, a match is set
to the fine mesh, and it begins to burn
faintly in the darkening dome.

And as the pressure of night increases
the mantle gives off a soft glow—
hangs radiant, a filigree of bright yellow.

The Japanese Gardener

The Japanese gardener
who keeps the river
is working hard today

He has raked
the entire bay
neatly

except for a small patch
near the centre

which he has trowelled
smooth   perfectly
smooth

Now just wait

and he will probably
move
that sailboat

into the stillness

for a mountain

Corellas Roosting

i

Corellas settling—
their voices softening with
the softening light.

ii

Strangely musical—
the white corellas roosting
in Windjana Gorge.

iii

Hauntingly at dusk
in the gums along the gorge—
white corellas call.

Irises

i
The grey water tank—
how vividly it sets off
the mauve irises!

ii
Purple irises ...
I rather prefer the ones
that Vincent painted.

Poppy

i
Needing ironing—
these recently unfolded
red poppy petals.

ii
Ah, such a vivid
impression—and with only
four petals, poppy!

She Enters with Flowers

for Liz McKenzie

She enters with flowers, roses
in their European opulence,
pastel-pink and partly open,

and places them in a vase,
a squat stoneware bottle
laying blue in the lacquer

of the dark hardwood table.
Independent of intention, her hands
brush the blooms into a loose

lolling order. This tenderness,
this elegance, elsetimes honoured
as 'feminine'. Elizabeth.

She enters with flowers,
unsettles the room with roses.
Unable to work, I watch

a white, pin-head spider
parachute from the petals.
Halting midair, it hangs

against the crazed face
of the blue-glazed clay,
its cordage caught on a thorn.

Blue Jug

It is nothing flash, the pale blue plastic jug
on my desk. But how beautifully it holds
those two loose-petalled pastel-pink roses and
that cluster of blazing-red pollen-lit gum blossom.
How it brightens my room, my mood, as I write,
reminding me of the things I am closeted from,
of that gungurru drooping its slender branches
over a wall by the footpath I walked this morning.

Through the jug's translucent plastic I see
a shadow of the stems submerged in the water,
the water I sweetened with a pinch of sugar.
Oh, for a palette to accompany my pen! Look
—those astonishing severed florescent stems,
sucking the clear cordial from the blue jug
to sustain their lolly colours and scents
—and that pint-sized big-handled part-frosted jug
that offered itself in the place of a vase.
Hard to imagine it being used for anything,
really, that jubilant jug—anything except
flowers, which of course I need not imagine,
it being presently packed with stamens and petals
there on my desk as (as I have said) I write.

It is the stuff of still life that stills life,
distils it to a hurrah and a hush. Such
gladness, such glory! If only I had a goldfish
I would plop it in to swim among the stalks.
I picture it easily, the small Buddha-bellied
bug-eyed fish. I fancy it wafting about
in the aquarium that was a jug that is a vase,
pilfering fire from the fiery eucalypt flowers,
fluttering silk scarves in the soft blue haze.

Escape

Confined by my work,
I look out my writing-room window
at the almond tree.
Through my binoculars, I observe
textured bark, tattered blooms, in 3D!

Bars

If only the words
and the ideas would connect,
I could get out, out!
Oh behold, now the bamboos
have barred my study window!

Impression

This could be Egypt, they could be gods:
three white ibises standing on a sand bar.
One preens its plumes, another peers
along the river, while the third steps
to the shallows to probe among the lilies.
This is not the Nile. There are no gods
but God. Yet how striking the impression:
this could be Egypt, they could be gods!

Snapping Things

Reeds picket the bank, form a brake,
pen the wild ducks, ripple and wake.

I am not one to make a noise,
but they swing to, detect my poise:

Shatter the water with their wings,
whistle to the air, snapping things.

Pink Fan Triggerplants

Who sets the heart for wonder?
What triggers the spring of praise?

Look! In a tumble of pink on the scree,
triggerplants—primed with pollen,

hammers cocked. Like the children,
I kneel to touch the heart of a flower.

Coots

Because it acts like a magnet on the eyes,
a strip of white adhesive tape
along the ridge of the nose
is a most effective disguise.

Coots knew this when masks were still in vogue
and long before nylon stockings
had been invented. A white beak
set in complete black
and running between the eyes
to the crown of the head
is standard wear for a coot.

So when a dabchick is beaten up
and the question ripples around the lake,
'Which one of the coots did it?'
the victim invariably has to admit:
'I only noticed his beak!'

Circles

Alongside the crop,
swept in the forest leaf-litter,
these little circles ...
Are the sand-bathing quails party
to the alien-landings hoax?

Pelicans

They look the part
the proud pelicans flocking
to play lacrosse.
But with their flash pink racquets
they catch better than they toss!

Telling Tales

After Kenneth Grahame's *The Wind in the Willows*

i

The frog on the road—
excited by tales telling
the exploits of Toad.

ii

Bold as Mister Toad
but not nearly as puffed up—
the frog on the road.

Farm Frogs

i

The dam at dusk—
two or three motorbike frogs
start revving up.

ii

Having a track meet
by the farm dam at midnight—
the motorbike frogs.

Mosquito Meditations

I
Koan

i

A mosquito koan—
What is the point of the sound
of one hand clapping?

ii

I just enlightened
a mosquito to the meaning
of a famed Zen koan!

II
Applause

i

Only you could rouse
such applause so late at night,
singing mosquito.

ii

Bow out, mosquito,
with the sound of my applause
in your puny ears!

III
Friendship

i

Keen to be my friend,
are you, little mosquito?
Okay, give me five!

ii

Oh dear, never mind ...
it wasn't your blood anyway,
little mozzie mate.

Dinner Bell

That dainty tinkle
from the cat's bell:

Dinner, friends,
will soon be served!

Welcome Swallows at Murdoch University

To this foreboding place,
where students learn through poems
of a season called Spring,
two swallows have come to make a home.

Too unimportant to be noticed
and too unconscious to care,
they skim through the rafters
and weave through the air.

At the end of one rafter
they dab mud for a nest:
it is the only spot
where they come to rest.

Who else would have dared
such a simple, untidy thing
here in the walkway
of the West Academic Wing?

Colour

A smoky colour,
the sort of colour you might
puff at bees before
robbing their hive of honey—
the white daisy's underside.

Enticement

To encourage
the picking of its flowers
the marri tree
offers some viewers a set
of last year's wooden vases!

The Radish

The radish
in the vegetable patch
has gone to seed.

It has grown big and unruly.
It has reached up
beyond its strength

and has fallen sideways
like a tree uprooted
after a strong wind.

It lies across the path,
a tangle of stems
and mauve flowers.

The flowers have turned
their faces to the sun
and among them three cabbage moths

flutter and settle
settle and flutter
and will not fly away—

as if I had nothing
better to do
than watch them all day.

While Watering Vegetables

In the silence of twilight
suddenly there is
a stuttering of white.

Cabbage moths,
flushed from hiding,
fluster in the fading light.

Of a million things
wonder is also
a winking of wings.

They settle again,
havened in my harvest,
until only one remains

scintillating
above the broad beans

like the evening star
above the quiet earth.

Shell

Life is no jewel
to the sea

How unconsciously
it must have cast this shell
this white spiral-shell
onto the beach years ago

Its owner died quickly
leaving the house quite empty
except for a ghost
of a smell, which lingered
about the empty stair-well

Without haste
the wind set to work:

Whispered, snickered,
incited the sand
to a sullen fury—
till every grain
on the beach
had raised its grit
to grind the fragile walls

It lies now a house in ruins:

Nothing left but a newel
jagged with the stumps
of several steps

Crabbing

Lights float above the blackness
and sometimes a voice drifts in.

We, too, wade into the water
made cold by the warm night.

Mud sucks at our shoes,
swirls up like ink about our legs.

My friend in his soft-rubber thongs
we comfort with the thought of cobbler.

His wife carries the tilly-lamp.
We huddle in the sanctuary of light,

fearful of what might lurk just out of sight.
Like moths, small fish bunt

blindly against my bare legs.
But the estuary is empty of crabs.

In vain we wander through this wet wilderness
in search of blue manna.

We wallow through the water, joke and
jump when imagination claws our ankles.

Once we saw a large crab
(like a straight-edge or a white bone)

with its arms outstretched
to embrace any threat

flicker ghost-like from our circle of light
into the infinite dark.

Squid Haiku

i
Squinting at an ink
blot on the pier ... what's it mean,
this squid Rorschach test?

ii
Luminous, the green
mascara the captured squid
has put on for death.

iii
In shock from the hook
that turned it into live bait,
the squid gently sinks ...

iv
Ink blot on the pier—
read no more into it than
the death of a squid.

Should I Fall and Fail to Rise

i

Early in the morning,
before the wind takes up its broom,
you can see where claws
have carved cuneiform runes
into the curve and crest
of the dunes.

Sandcrabs, secretive in sunlight,
solaced by sand,
scavenge the beach by starlight.

Had I the courage, I would come
alone in the dark
to watch their mechanical rituals.

ii

Above the wet sand, there are holes
asterisked by claws.
Creatures governed by laws

as eldritch and rich as the sea,
laws they neither know nor need to learn,
hide in the dark, spurn

both sunlight and me.
I finger a tunnel, scoop the sand
gingerly with an endoskeletal hand.

And suddenly, angrily, there
it is—the sandcrab,
boxbodied like a hansomcab.

iii

High on the beach, the exoskeleton
of a blue manna crab.
Its crablife has crept sideways
into death's sea, leaving
a frail cenotaph
to bleach and crack in the sun.

iv

I gaze at the ocean. Out there
armoured in carapace and claw
roam crabs as long and as hard
as the bones in my arm.

v

Look carefully, and you will see
the shells walk. Hermit crabs
inhabit the reef—housed
in periwinkles and whelks
tritons and topshells.

And there, in high conical shells,
several crabs waver
with the wash of the water.

Like initiates at a secret ritual,
they dance in their white hats—
the ku klux klansmen
of the crustacean world.

vi

Tiny, translucent-red crabs
hide in the branching coral,
waiting for the debris
of decaying fish.

vii

Camouflaged in combat green
rockcrabs scuttle into crevices.
Waves smash over them, but they remain
immovable. With their periscope eyes
and their bathysphere bodies
they are the ancient world's answer
to science fiction.

viii

Wielding its smallclaw like a broadsword,
holding its shovelclaw like a shield:
the sandcrab. Unless you kill it, it will not yield.

ix

In the sands of the beach
in the rocks by the shore
and on the ocean's floor
crabs click in crustacean speech.

As I walk this beach alone
I begin to realise
should I fall and fail to rise
they will whittle me to the bone.

Menace

It's not just the colours,
the burnt-out blacks and blazing oranges

It's not just the flying,
the buzzing wings and erratic barging

It's also the walking,
the stop-starting and upstart dart-poking

With all the while the wings
rigid and out-jutting from the thorax ...

Yes, above all, the wings,
those at-the-ready wind-whetted switchblades

Wings angled like the arms
of a bad man, a madman, hands on hips

Elbows crooked defiant,
daring any hothead to take him on—

The spider-hunting wasp
roving on and around the garden rocks.

Black Cockatoos

As they like all creatures
came originally from Mind,
not matter, the cockatoos
are part of the supernatural.

And hearing a large flock
croak and snarl and creak
in the crowns of the gums,
I realise just how easily

a man could mistake them
for black spirits, demented
and dreadful, if he did not
know that 'black' as a state

of the heart belongs sadly
solely to humans and demons.

Walking Past Nightfall

I peer to where
I think the farmhouse should be.
How easily
I left it in the daylight,
left it without
globes glowing in the windows.
A mopoke mopes
on the far side of the flames,
flames I forsake
for the sake of returning.
A strand of wire
telegraphs news of the fence.
I make my way
through the featureless paddock.
The moon batters
an eyelash but gives no light.
Moaning frogs moan
in chorus to mark the marsh.
Nearby I hear
the heavy hollow thumping
of kangaroos—
kangaroos crashing about!
Can they see me
as well as I can't see them?
Oh, now listen …
the cattle, too, are pounding
in panic at my presence!

That Bird

for Zenon Pirga

Hiking in the Avon Valley
I saw a wedge-tailed eagle
circle like a bomber-plane
unsure of its target. It flapped

periodically to keep its height,
pumping the air between pauses.
Then suddenly it hit a thermal
and spiralled up, hanging

in the hammock of its wings.
Without thought of me and
without my thought, the eagle
edged into and out of my vision.

That bird—so utterly other.
All day, it hung on the chain
of my thoughts like a crucifix.
In camp, I imagined it roosting

somewhere in the darkness,
blood on its talons, meat
in its gut. Like its prey,
it was bound for oblivion.

It was going into death without
knowing or being known. But by
this poem (imperfectly, temporarily)
I lift that bird above its destiny.

Hawk

Hunched in an overcoat of feathers
a hawk on the high wire,
like a snapshot of a shrug

As easily as he wields the wind in his wings
and clamps small creatures in his claws,
he sheds the world from his shoulders

White-faced Heron

By the river the white-faced heron—
geisha refinement and deportment,

Buddhist reflection and detachment,
ninja readiness and commitment,

haijin restiveness and engagement
—carries on like a white-faced heron.

Casuarina, Walyunga

The tree by the river
is a casuarina, a sheoak that rises
from a reticulation of exposed roots
fanning like rivulets over the flatland
that dries in summer to a mere dampness.

The tree by the river
is a river of wood
pouring into the air
through a tangle of tributaries.

It is a spider
spinning a wooden web
over the black clay
to catch the beetle-backed stones.

It is a dark place
that dugites are slithering into.

The tree by the river
is a vertical glacier
upheld by a horizontal delta.

It is a congealed artery
clotted to a network of varicose veins.

It is a giant nerve
synapsed to the earth.

It is an enormous amoeba
flowing into pseudopods.

The tree by the river
is an axle
radiating bent, bifurcating spokes.

It is the south pole
drawing longitudinal lines
that wobble into latitude.

It is a conductor rod
struck at the base by forked lightning.

It is a powerhouse
feeding sunlight to the earth
through a gridwork of cables.

The tree by the river
is a cartographer
charting the concentric
contour lines of the land.

It is a conservationist
enmeshing the soil
against the eroding water.

It is a constructionist
scaffolding the ground for renovations.

The tree by the river
is a fisherman
casting a circular net
on a site where minnows will swim in winter.

It is a tribal elder
renewing the rituals of initiation,
cicatrising the chest of the black earth.

It is the Rainbow Serpent
giving birth to thin black snakes.

The tree by the river
is a lubra
knotting her slender toes to the earth,
lifting her supple arms to the wind.
She is weeping, tossing her hair and
wailing for the warriors
whose bones lie in the red loam
not far from the running water,
the young warriors
who will never return to Walyunga.

Waugal, Upper Swan

From any spot along the bank
you can see the spirit-snake
slip by—the Waugal,
the wakeful river's Dreaming.

It bucks above or skirts about
the rocks, slides by, gleaming,
each sud a white scale.
Watch all winter and you will

not see the end of its tail.
Yet come midsummer
the serpent's flesh will rot away
leaving only a rubble of vertebrae.

Ibises, Sydney

In Hyde Park, white ibises
wander among mynahs, sparrows
and pigeons. Their plumage,
granted, is grimed by smog
and their bills toss scraps
tossed by tourists. Still,
there they are, in the heart
of the city—white ibises!

With their presence, the park
becomes pristine and primitive.
Look, a small flock probes
the marsh where the fountain
will be. Nearby, arm crooked
to the shape of his boomerang,
a hunter notes the breeze as
he watches those slender necks

bend and straighten and bend.

Sighting

On visiting the Bull Ranges with a traditional landowner

Pluck out the detecting eye,
break off the pointing finger,
shut up the exclaiming cry—
if only somehow I could!

But it's too late to stifle
myself now or stop my friend,
who snatches up his rifle
and follows swiftly after

the wallabies I sighted,
the small wild rock wallabies
whose survival I blighted
simply because I saw them

and cried aloud, delighted.

Wedgetails

Disillusionment—
seeing again and again
wedgetail eagles
in the outback, not soaring
but just perching on roadkill.

Bull and Bird

The water dripping
from the muzzle of the bull
spoils the reflection
of the masked plover wading
between its great muddy hooves.

Throat Notes

i
Buzz-note beeping—
a juvenile zebra finch
gapes for feeding.

ii
A squawking split-
note from a finch with a fuzz-
box in its throat!

iii
Tibetan monks,
fledgling finch, also utter
a double note!

iv
Are you gagging
or just throat-singing, feeding
fledgling finches?

v
Your throat-singing,
immature finch, is making
your mum throw up!

Zoom

An overload
of loveliness, this landscape.
I isolate
several sections with my lens
to make the beauty stand out.

Focus

Only as the lens
of the camera segments
it into oblongs
does the sight of the outback
landscape become becoming.

Native Pears

Unopened, the nuts of the native pear
are pale-green plumb-bobs.
They are the bodies of twig-necked ducks.
They are moulds for winged seeds.

As they dry to grey
stretch marks mar their Buddha bellies.

Opened, the nuts are
long-eared rabbits resting on their haunches.
They are wooden-winged butterflies.
They are castanets that cannot click.

Shift Focus

Hakea laurina

Naming is mostly metaphor. So with the Pincushion Hakea
the botanist pre-empted an image for flowers the poet
had yet to discover: blooms composed of stiff pistils pinned
in a scarlet cushion of compact petals. The bush, named
from the flower, named in turn from a correspondence.

Now shift focus to the fruit. The nut of the hakea
is a hard cocoon, a wooden chrysalis. Within, a pupa swells
on the plant's sap, matures into an indigo-black imago.
Fully winged, the butterfly bides its time, waiting
for drought or fire to crack the case for its release.

As a footprint through fossilisation leaves an imprint
in stone, so the imago in departure leaves an image
of wings—their perfect, candle-flame shapes—
on the paired planes of wood where the chrysalis gapes.

Karri

That tree that thankfully is not
500 fence posts or 50 polished tables
or 20 bookcases crammed with books

—that tree that could be anything
(except alive) a skilled man
might sensibly conceive it to be

—that tree that stands in the air
like a condominium, crowned
with cranes and scaffolding

—*that* tree is unsettled by flowers,
those small plumes of white blossom
fluttering from the tonnes of wood.

Jarrah

The calm of the forest amplifies
a faint, flat tintinnabulation.
The jarrah trees are just in bud
and the buds are beginning to burst.

Like miniature bracken fronds,
the filaments of each flower unfurl,
forcing open the operculum, the cap
that covers the nascent blossom.

As they fall, the floral caps
(small as the drumstick heads
of matches) strike the dry leaf-
litter on the forest floor,

punctuate the stillness
with an arrhythmic percussion.
Like the particles of a sun shower,
they parachute at random

to the ground. One lands on the tip
of a grasstree leaf, balances
on the sharp leaf-shaft like
a bamboo hat on a lanky oriental.

Marri with Nuts

After rain
sometimes gumnuts
—the big-bowled,

boldly-rimmed
nuts of the marri
—smoulder

as if packed
with tobacco
and set alight.

Or, which is
more beautiful,
as if each nut

were a thurible,
a wooden censer,
wafting incense.

Indeed, this
green-robed tree
is a thurifer

unconsciously
praising God
most consciously

through me.

Western Yellow Robin

When the Almighty
spoke yellow-bellied robins
into bright being
and told them to multiply,
he already knew
I would observe this robin,
this gentle-grey bird
too shy to wear its colour
on its petite breast,
this yolk-yellow-under bird
drawn from the forest
by the feather-grey and -fine
smoke of my campfire—
and he also foreknew that
I would by virtue
of his implanted image
want to celebrate
and recreate this bird by
speaking it into a poem.

Burning

Hemmed in by fire
the gecko on the great log
crawls still higher.
I reach out, but it regards
my hand on par with the pyre.

Burning Off

A giant grasstree—
magnificent, though it's not
alive anymore.
It is a thatched Zulu hut.
Firing it, I feel like a Boer.

Summer Robins

i
A daring colour
for Australian summers,
red-vested robin!

ii
Robins in summer—
even the female now seems
alarmingly bright!

iii
Unwise to say it
in bushfire season, but aren't
the robins striking!

Imagine a Tree in a Paddock

Imagine a tree in a paddock

Choose any shape of trunk
consider a thousand textures of bark:
but polish bright and smooth
a band a few feet from the ground

remember the burnishing of hides

And sketch however you wish
the casual proportions of the canopy:
but rule a straight line
at the base to stop the leaves

remember the secateuring of teeth

In the Interim

That paddock the farmer is ripping
will soon bristle with seedlings.
Imagine it. Saplings queuing up
on the pasture! Then a forest. Yes.

For many years before the felling,
a forest of blue gums or pines.
This paradox: a forest arising from
a want of timber! In the interim

see how the man with the tractor,
methodical as a child with a crayon,
is drawing thick chocolate lines
on the green sheet of the paddock.

Striking, those dark scribbles,
parallel and contoured to the hill!

Shooting

The rainwater tank is rusted and tipped on its rings
like a fanned accordion. Rabbits have made a warren
beneath it. Diggings and droppings surround it.

I am sitting on a rock behind the trunk of a river gum,
rifle cocked and propped against the tree, waiting.
Sometimes I peer past the wood and see only pasture.

Now there is a mallee root where no root was before.
It is hunched greyly beside the black mouth of a burrow.
I sight and fire. It spins back and sprawls dead.

I collect the carcass and settle back behind the tree.
Beside me, clear water skids by in a shallow stream bed.
A pair of twenty-eight parrots fly down to bathe.

They stand belly deep and dunk themselves repeatedly.
They fly into the river gum and nip the flower buds,
dropping them onto me, as if I were renowned and worthy.

A robin hops around the roots, warming me with images
of fire. A pardalote clings to a cluster of leaves.
A wagtail whirls like a dervish. Far off, crows caw.

Since first they saw me, the cattle have been slowly
moving towards me. Now they are grazing beside
the derelict tank, making it too dangerous to shoot.

Young Hereford heifers. A baker's dozen. They meander
closer. I keep still. At three metres they stop
and all nonchalance disappears. They bunch together

in a half-circle, facing me. I wait. A rosella alights
to drink. As it dips its bill, a cow steps onto a twig.
The bird flinches but does not fly away. One beast

ventures from the mob, snuffling me with great snorts.
Its pink-grey plasticine muzzle is covered with beads
of condensation. It stares at me, nodding its head

like Mr Squiggle. It nudges the butt of my gun, rasps
the polished wood with its tongue. Suddenly the rosella
flies up, startling the herd. They bolt and prance.

The spell of my presence is broken. The red roan bull
cloistered in the far clover bellows, beckoning them
with an urgency they can extinguish but not experience.

I start out for home, carrying my gun and my kill.

Red Gum

The wood is green so the saw
is quick. I rock the blade
in the groove and the chain

gouges in, churning sawdust
onto my boots. Another cut,
another cylinder of firewood.

And suddenly resin spills
copious and crimson from
a canal in the sapwood. Oh,

staining the blond heartwood,
red gum, the tree's namesake,
vivid and viscous as murder.

A Farewell to Roosters

i

Leaving the country—
no need to leave the hens, but
what of the roosters?

ii

Strutting and crowing
are fine in the city—but
not for *real* roosters!

iii

Even for nothing
no one will take them, our
resplendent roosters.

iv

I'll hear it again,
perhaps, but not from these throats—
cockcrow at cockcrow.

v

Brighter than their combs—
bantam rooster blood before
it clots on the blade.

Hawk Hovering

Is it gluttony
or hunger that goads the hawk
to be hunting still?
The sun is so low the bird
is buoyed and buoyant with light.

Return

On the verandah
at twilight ... wondering if
the kite will return
once again to the pale sky
above the blue gum saplings.

Ospreys

Further back, they looked like shags
roosting in the dead tree: two ospreys.
They own the river from here to the sea.

I have seen them pirouette
on the toe of the air
high above the cliffs
that hedge the river,
waiting for the flicker of a shadow
or the glimmer of a ripple
in the brown water below.

Fish-eagles:
strange thermals lift the heart
at the mere thought of them.

Left Foot

That white-faced heron
on the grassed bank
is paddling the water
with its bony left foot.

An up-and-down flurry
as if rinsing some muck
from its orange toes.
A little loud splashing.

Then stillness, silence.
Stare. Head, beak, this
way and that, as a blunt
knife across the steel.

Zilch. Step. Stop. Step.
Again, the spindly leg
stretching out, poised
as if in blessing.

Another brisk dabble
as if to suds the water.
Ah! Startled, a minnow
darts from cover. Stab!

Stints

In a plane inches above the estuary water,
in close but changing proximity,
a symmetry, a squadron of stints
reconnoitre a stretch of shoreline

They settle in the rotting seaweed
that lolls against the shore

They snipe at kelp-flies,
prod and pick
at unimaginable tiny things
thriving in the sweet stench

Stints, in the last of our summer,
gathering strength
against the call of Siberia

Moorhen

Moorhen, merehen
on the manicured moors
around the artificial mere

Dusky moorhen
red-beaked, pierce-beaked
among the dull-billed teal

The last creation
in the dusk of the fifth day:
bearing on its forehead

the mould, the snub
of God's thumb
as He plied and pressed the beak home

Agreement

i
Yes, stilt, attributes
unrelated to your legs
are noteworthy, too.

ii
Yes, regrettably,
your legs hardly represent,
poor stilt, the real you.

iii
Yes, I agree, stilt:
it's objectification
of a ghastly sort.

iv
Yes, it's unfair, stilt,
that the avocet avoids
the stigma of 'stilt'!

Croaking

i
On the second beat
a second frog also croaks—
chill winter evening.

ii
Antiphonal—
two frogs calling either end
of the puddle.

Fish and Lily

i
A café patron—
the goldfish loafing in the shade
of the lily-pad.

ii
Goldfish and water
lily flower—who gave whom
that pastel colour?

Realism

A surreal bubble
rising to break the image
of a tree-fern leaf
filmed upon the pond surface—
that sluggish fantail goldfish.

Overflow

Where the water is
overflowing from the pond,
floating waterweed
has gathered against the rim
as if to view something grim.

Oak, Oakover Homestead

The oak (grant me this
conceit) is a herd
of elephants. They are
all in there, the pachyderms,
packed in that pillar
of wood and piled
upon one another's
shoulders. Those higher up
are snorkelling out
their trunks—enormous trunks
stretching out
and dropping down
to sweep along
the grass-sweet ground.
Look at them,
the English-oak-elephants,
snuffling about for acorns!

Willow

The willow is a fisherman,
and highly successful at that.
I refer not to the rods
it rests towards the river
in winter, but to the strings
of fish it shoulders in summer.
The tree teems with fish—
small green minnows strung
by their heads, dangling
one below the other, some
twisting in the dry breeze.

Almond

The almond tree about mid-autumn becomes
(wait—savour it!) a Rhode Island rooster,
feathered in russets and reds.

It struts in its season about the backyard
bestowing feathers on lawn and flower bed,
displaying its finery to the evergreen lemon.

When the wind, that old fox, is on the prowl
the conceited cock flaps and crows, all
puffed up with bravado and banter.

It spars at the air with its twiggy spurs.
The coxcomb! Inevitably, I wake near winter
to find the fox has taken it by the throat

and shaken its feathers off. But I'm not
alarmed. For the almond is a phoenix fowl,
replenishing its plumes each spring.

The Brobdingnagian Banana

The banana tree is
a Brobdingnagian bricklayer.
He has suspended an enormous

plumb-bob from a green rope
to read the lean of things,
to plot the perpendicular. There is

a beauty in this, too—a unity
of utility and artistry,
a melding of function and form.

For the plumb-bob is made
of beaten-copper bracts
layered within each other—

large leaf-sheets
cupped curving and diminishing
to a core of nothing. And

between each sheet (observe
how the top one is loosened)
there is a row of golden trumpets

summoning the swift honeyeaters,
those feathered Lilliputians,
with a fanfare of nectar.

Tree-Fern

The tree-fern is an orchestra
playing a pastorale. Glorious
the meticulous melodies, the green
movements. On centre stage
the soloist lifts his violin—
light on the line of the neck,
the tuning pegs, the perfect
carved curl—poised to begin.

Sunflower

The sunflower, evolutionists
will be elated to learn,
is in the process of becoming

an enormous insect. Vegetable
to animal—a veritable
missing link! The sunflower.

It is an almost-blowfly
watching the wondrous world
through a compound eye.

Maize Metamorphosis

Though it may seem
amazing, most maize
plants become poultry
by summer's end.

A stand of sweet
corn, when it's
dry as a shock,
becomes a flock

of leghorn hens.
They're shy, don't
like to be seen,
but turn your back

and you'll learn
what I mean.
Listen. Already
they're scratching

about for greens.
And did you note
how they wait—
simply won't

begin to fossick—
until the wind
wields its trowel
to smooth the sound

of their work?
Och, the furtive fowls!
How could they have
learnt such a lurk?

Wine Country

Playtime and the children
are charged with games
and loud alliances.

Beside the school the vines
have linked arms
among the rowdy dandelions.

Transformation

I fumble beneath
the broody bantam.

Ah, as I fancied—
an egg's gone fluffy!

I draw it cheeping
into the chill air.

Chook and Children

It never recovered from motherhood, the black hen.
It went clucky, hoarded eggs, hatched chickens
and turned vicious. Months later and still
it fluffs to a fury and hurls itself at our legs.

A plump, feathered lance, it draws blood
from our fatted calves. The children are afraid
to collect the eggs. Terror roams the chook-run.
Today, it hurtled at my son as he reached

into the feed-bin. He fended it off with the lid,
held like a shield at his shins, until I arrived
with a tomato stake to beat it back. It baulked,
squawked and flapped a swift retreat. The children

rejoice. Oh-ho, father with justice in his fist!
Ah-ha, the chicken-livered chook! Under the apple
tree the fowl fluffs up, shakes off its fright.
Looking on, my daughter says, 'Deserves him right!'

Poem about Freedom

I am sitting in the shade
of the lemon tree, trying to write
a poem about freedom. But

my son is swinging in the almond,
calling, 'Dad, look at this! Dad!'
The day conspires to distract me

from things I have designated
important. On a branch
arching over me, a lemon's

green rind is yielding to yellow.
Near my feet, a hornet
is hurtling sand from a hole

set in a clear space
between the rootbound and budless
chrysanthemums. In the apple tree

the fruits' round cheeks
are powdered with rouge
and a parrot is summoning its mate

to a feast. Now my daughter
crams her rag doll
in the cane chair beside me and

places in its lap a sprig of mint.
Bruised by her clumsy hands
it smells so clean and sweet.

Concerning Crusader Bugs

I
Pilgrimage

With wings slung like shields
on their backs, crusader bugs
pilgrimage through the holy land
of my garden.

II
For My Son

Crusader bugs lurk
in dark crevices of bark.

Like a Saracen,
I hunt them out for my son,

the Emir of my heart.

III
Escutcheon

Sable, a saltire tenne—
on a black field,
St Andrew's cross
in orange emboss.

All day I have studied heraldry
just to blazon this shield
shaped by a crusader bug's wings.

Correspondence

As a scrap of string
snagged on a rail

hangs down yet,
because of the wind,

bows buoyantly back,
so a wasp's hind legs

dangle as it flies.

Plumage

It appears
to be plumed

the grass spider
scurrying from

the wet white
feather duster

of my hose.
Look closely.

Its abdomen
is plumped up

with spiderlings.
Unsettled

they ruffle.
Several scatter

to the lawn
erratic

rickety
like blown down.

Emergence

Cicadas have left their cuticles
clinging to the daisy stems:

brown shells, burst at the back
of the thorax. Emergent, one

is exquisitely veined in aqua,
its wings soft as membrane.

Soon its juices will blacken
and its wings become cellophane.

Then it will tick, metallic
and fast, like an engine cooling.

Gravity

i
At work even
on a resting dragonfly's wings—
gravity's pull.

ii
A trace of a bow
in each of the four wing-blades
of the dragonfly.

Target

i
Slightly off-centre—
the bullseye in the target
hung by the spider.

ii
Another insect
has a shot at the bullseye
of the web target.

Long Legs

i

Are they prosthetics,
the legs daddy-long-legs left
hanging on the door?

ii

Dear mummy-long-legs
was so smitten with daddy
she gobbled him up!

iii

Poor daddy-long-legs
learnt too late the body snatcher
was mummy-long-legs.

Action Shot

Nearly as quick as
the shutter, the grasshopper
leaving the photo.
Look, a blur of springing legs
and a burst of spinning sand!

Shutter Lag

My camera
on super macro setting
shutters too late.
It misses the grasshopper
and catches instead its leap!

Dance

Pied cormorants festoon the dead trees
that jut from the steep dunes.
A white egret labours to the air,
croaking protest. On the wooded side
of the river, a sacred kingfisher
glints among the greenery
like a scrap of blue torn from the sky
and blown between the branches.
Fish burst from the startled water
in our wake. An osprey casually pirouettes
onto the stage of my sight. Briefly,
on wind and water, bird and boat
perform a glissading *pas de deux*. Look!
I say, See the bird? Hear the fish?
But my little daughter is lost
in dance. She lilts from side
to side, accentuating the rhythm
of the canoe as I alternate
my weight against the paddle.

Poised on a Premonition

I sit waiting for a fish
to telegraph its presence to my fingers.
There is no communication.
Are there fish in the depths? Perhaps
they are poised on a premonition
of death. My son jerks his line,
imitating the old men at the end
of the jetty. My little daughter,
resenting her mother's restraining hand,
dangles a stone-weighted stocking
into the water. From the far side of the estuary,
the *kek-kek* cry of a kestrel
fires at us. What, I wonder, has it killed?

'I've got one, Dad!' Clumsily,
he pulls in his line: a small bream
whirls against its will
upward to the suffocating air—
its life a thread of silver, unravelling
through the clear water.
It is small; but my son will not spare it.
As it dries and dies on the jetty,
a faint, rainbowing iridescence
disappears from its head.

I feel a bite, bring in a trumpet fish.
It hangs from my line like a chime
fluttering in the winds of death.
It trumpets softly, as if crooning endearments,
as I jiggle the hook from its mouth.
I hold it to my daughter's ear.
'He's talking to me.' She turns to touch
its eye. 'He likes me, doesn't he, Dad?'

Unnoticed

Rather like poets
the brown leafy seadragons—
unnoticed until
their deaths—and then only if
some wave washes them ashore.

Warrior Monk

Short sword ready,
the heron warrior monk
contemplates what
it fancies shimmers beneath
the world floating at its feet.

A Good Night

The mulies are in the harbour,
shoals of them, teeming unseen
in the opaque sea. On the wharf,

in rubber boots and yellow raincoats,
a team of professional fishermen
lure the fish with food and light.

They have hung a lantern, hissing
incessant warning, just above
the quilted surface of the quiet water;

and they have strewn pollard—
the pollen grains, the yeasty smell—
on the water, below the lamp,

above the submerged net—an iron hoop
looped with mesh, long and tapering
like a windsock. Near the net,

a ship shifts uneasily. Its rope,
a catenary from prow to bollard,
strains and straightens. Bilge-water

spouts from the hull. On the wharf,
an enormous, enclosed conveyor-belt
rolls on its gantry. Grain

cascades into the hold. Behind
the ship, winnowed by the wind
and stretching as far as the shining

of the harbour lights, barley husks
form a yellow slick on the black
water. Between the lamp and the net

the mulies, the bait-fish, swirl
like long-bodied moths. At a command,
the men hoist the net. It is a crucible

bubbling with molten silver.
Poured out, the fish separate
into small, oblong ingots. A young man

smooths them into shallow crates,
ready for freezing. But the fish
are not ready. Frenzied,

they flick and twist, scales flying off
like sequins from a silver purse.
Their gills gape, the red frills

clogged by air. Their mouths gasp,
transparent lips extended
like trumpets, blaring, 'O! O!'

The conveyor-belt and the bilge-pump
drone a duet to drown Death's reveille.
The ship's rope heaves and relaxes.

In a child's hand, a line twitches
like a caught nerve. In the crates,
the fish have gone off the boil

and lay eternally still. The men
lower the net again. 'Gonna be a good
night,' smiles one man, his hair
spangled with scales, like confetti.

Four Men

The contraption is like a small
merry-go-round at a country fair:
five cradles at the end of five arms
which meet at a hub and turn

on an upright axle. Inverted
stirrups are welded to the sides
of each cradle. A man stands at,
and a lamb lies in, four of the cradles.

Four lambs on the merry-go-round.
The fourth man tosses one off. Spin
round. The first man lifts one up
and lays it on its back.

Much as a gynaecologist might
hook a woman's legs out and back,
he hooks the lamb's hocks
in the stirrups. Spin round.

The second man injects a poison
for parasites, jabbing the needle
in the sternum, and clips a piece
from an ear. No sound. Spin

round. The third man holds
a pair of sharp shears. He pinches
the fleece beside the tail
and snips. A crisp, fibrous sound,

like cutting cloth. It is an art
to cut no deeper than the depth
of the skin. Blood spurts out,
a thin jet, as from a water-pistol;

or, thinner yet, like a spray of juice
from an orange as it is peeled.
From the root of the tail, he cuts
along the side of the anus,

the vulva, skinning the lamb
alive. The exposed meat films
with blood. Barely a struggle.
Only a single, bleating scream

with the first cut. Mulesing,
they call it, and do it to safeguard
the flock from fly-strike.
Between the third man's boots,

shaped like a cowpat, a pool-pile
of coagulating blood wobbles
like a jelly. Snip. Spin round.
The fourth man slips a rubber ring

on the tail. (With a ram lamb,
he clamps another ring around
the scrotum—that little purse
from which no ewe will ever receive

conception's shining currency.)
Then he unhooks the legs
and dumps the lamb in the dirt.
Spin round. Begin again. It takes

barely one minute. Mulesing.
I jot a few notes. The four men
are uneasy. What will the townie
write? 'Y'aren't an animal libber,

are ya?' Banter among the blood
and bleating. I concede there is
no mercy in a death by maggots.
The last lamb hobbles, bellowing,

to its mother, a red glare
at its rear. The pasture is splotched
with crimson. 'They've got their
tail-lights on,' the third man grins,

wiping the blood from his hands.

Birth

Downhill from the herd,
a cow and her newborn calf.

The baby bull lies steaming
in a muddy puddle on the loam.

The cow nuzzles it,
rasps it roughly with her tongue.

A red rope of afterbirth
hangs in tandem with her tail.

Blood colours her urine.
Colostrum drips from her teats.

Wet and wonky, the calf
struggles to stand. Finally

on all fours, it wobbles
for a moment then collapses

as if a bullet had bludgeoned
its brain. Oh, this foreboding.

Dark Sky

The sky is dark, dark.
It's a fact. It's a figure.
I look out the window
at my heart. I look out.

In a bush in the rain
a small bird is fluffing
and fluttering. I watch it
briefly, then turn away.

What does it mean, that
buff-bellied thornbill
rejoicing in the steady rain
from the dark sky? What?

Bamboo Meditations

i
Despite emptiness,
the bamboo is oblivious
to every sadness.

ii
Encapsulated
in the Buddha bamboo canes—
only emptiness.

iii
Bamboo reflections—
pondering again the canes'
hidden emptiness.

iv
Today I could teach
even the Buddha bamboo
about emptiness.

Rose

The day after I cut it
I notice the white rose
in the pottery vase
on my desk start to wilt.

All day it has been
drooping lower and lower,
until now its small head
is hanging upside down,

lolling loose-haired
against the shoulder
of the vase, as if given
entirely to sorrow.

Happiness

A small green bird is hopping
up the grey trunk of a river gum.
The tree leans toward the water.
A duck floats on its reflection.

The climbing bird knocks a fleck
of bark into the water. The duck
inspects it then paddles away.
The Chinese poet Tu Fu wrote,

'After the laws of their being
all creatures pursue happiness.'
Watching the birds, the dragon-
flies, it occurs to me that Fu

is quite wrong. Apart from man,
all creatures simply *are* happy.
No duck ends the day with regret.
We alone aspire to something

Other. And we alone fall short.

Miscellaneous Haiku

1
A little breeze—
and lollipop kisses from
the red poppies.

2
Pale in my headlights
on the glistening road—a frog
hiccupping along!

3
In the stoneware bowl
after the small bird's bathing—
rainwater wobbling.

4
Over the humming
of the fridge, I hear again
a blue wren singing.

5
The polished surface—
a white egret hesitates
to put its foot down.

6
Making an 'M'
between them on the water—
the swimming ducks.

7
Sort of springy—
the kelpie trotting beside
the stilted sheep.

8
Boys, dragonflies—
from one rock to another
in the fast stream.

9
I'd be weeping too,
willow, if the sheep had given
me that basin cut!

10
No way out, but still
such a high and happy yell—
the frog in the well!

11
Unafraid, a finch
comes through my binoculars
into my presence.

12
Harbour pelicans—
judging by their beaks, the same
slant on everything.

13
The shimmering heat ...
to a shrinking puddle wasps
come shimmying down.

14
A cloudless day—
zebra finches peg themselves
to the clothesline.

15
Lunging right in
the shag before the garfish
leaping right out.

16
The garden bamboo ...
I am distracted by thoughts
of Japanese flutes.

17
Butterfly sprinkler—
beckoning by fluttering
a flock of finches.

18
Inconspicuous
but for the ripples—the nose
tip of a tortoise.

19
Evening daisy—
a peacock after courtship
closing its fan.

20
Uprightness and shine
hinder the little bird's hold
on the bamboo cane.

21
Violets in a vase—
one day of admiration
to finish them off.

22
As if its right eye
could be wrong, the cormorant
turns its left to me.

23
A scent so subtle
it put pollen on her nose
before she noticed.

24
I pause to pick
a poppy seeded in a crack
in the sidewalk.

25
Such fabulous poise—
the waterlily balancing
four saucers at once!

26
The climbing rose—
a tendril tugs my shirtsleeve
through the trellis.

27
The *thock* of my axe—
loose bark sloughs to uncover
both halves of a skink.

28
Soundless bullroarers—
the slender peppermint leaves
spinning as they fall.

29
Hard to explain if
we were seen—two men feeding
red ants to sundews.

30
A lemon blossom—
landing, a bee knocks off one
white waxen petal.

31
'Bye bye bird,' she says
and waves, as the little frog
leaps free of my hand.

32
Perhaps next year
they will notice bars and smells—
children at the zoo.

33
As if the sun's torch
had cut through the cloud's steel-plate—
wattles, blazed in gold.

34
Like catching a crab
in spawn—lifting a fern frond,
the spores spotted there.

35
Padding through puddles,
the dog drops its jaw ... slight wake,
the taste of water.

36
In the forest
something drops, stops with a thud.
A bird cries out.

37
One month of winter—
already the pallid cuckoos
are calling, calling.

38
Petunias—
playing their horns to my shoes
from the dry pot.

39
A bee is drinking
at the drip I meant to stop
from the garden tap.

40
Stepping out to stare
up at the stars ... a mopoke
calls from the forest.

41
Asymmetry—
bestowing on the lopped pine
a strange beauty.

42
Drifting away—
a discomforting feather
a dove dislodged.

43
Stoical until
the tenderness of my touch—
the fallen petal.

44
Flying off, the seeds
of the hakea nut leave
an imprint of wings.

Two Rivers

As they join, the Swan and Helena are hemmed
with a patchwork of paddocks and parks
where, in spring, birds come to court and mate.

Black ducks and moorhens navigate and nest
among reeds and bulrushes. Kingfishers
and parrots covet holes in river gums.

Honeyeaters and thornbills twist grass
and fluff among twigs and foliage. The fields
bloom with song. Even the drabbest birds

strew bright flowers from their throats.
Beneath the paperbarks, arum lilies
gather in their white habits like nuns

released from the convent of winter. And
bracken ferns raise their crosiers
to bless the opulent earth. People also

come. At King's Meadow Oval and Point Reserve
they plot the ground with picnic blankets
(radish red, broccoli blue, zucchini green)

like market gardeners growing happiness.
Men slap meat on barbecues; women rummage
through baskets; children bask on banks or

jump from jetties. And occasionally, with their
long leotard-white feet, canoeists perform
spurting *pas glissades* on the polished water.

Spring, Alfred Cove

This wildlife sanctuary: the last wetland on the Swan
River estuary. How long will it last? Some call it
wasteland, and few notice it at all. A patch of sedge

signals in semaphore to an inattentive world.
Samphires mat the mudflats, their bulbous stems
like strings of red and green rosary beads. Bulrushes

grow on a bank, their cylindrical bales of wool
bursting open from the season's rough, ripe handling.
With its numerous, invisible needles, the wind

knits the water plain and purled. Pelicans,
their wings unfurled, float fathoms above the cove,
caught in slow, wide eddies. Terns in turn

kamikaze the battleship-grey water, rise again
unhurt. A dozen black ducks at the water's edge
quack quietly as they dredge the sludge. Stilts

step on their reflections with their spindly,
backward-bending legs. Cormorants practise Tai Chi
on wireless and weathered fence posts. An egret

stands without a mate beside a beached boat.
Also alone, a greenshank hunts along the sandbars.
Soon others will come from Siberia,

charting their way by the changeless stars.

Wattle, Mundaring Weir

The wattle tree was once a battleship.
The mainmast, the cut of the sail,
the sound of the sea when the wind
is up—these many confirmations.
But most telling of all, the hammocks
slung haphazardly from the bark's
rigging. Pleasing, really, to ponder
the seedy crew snug in their bedding,
dreaming of piracies and plunder.
Given germination, each crew will
captain his own landlocked wattleship,
bombard spring with bursts of blossom.

Stamens

In the arboretum by the Collie River
Tasmanian blue gums drop their stamens.

Look, a loose thread on my sleeve,
a white hair on the back of my hand.

Filament and anther, each stamen is
thin and knobbed, as a butterfly's antenna.

As I sit hoping for egrets and herons,
this steady drizzle ... this lightness ...

And drifting up from the damp ribbons
of shed bark, that aroma of eucalyptus.

Breaking Out

A eucalypt bud is an incarceration of strong men—
boxers—cramped, bent double in a green locker-room
with a conical ceiling-cum-roof. Though they dislike
each other, they co-operate, set their shoulders

to the shelter's cover. They press and push, crack
the seal that holds the ceiling to the circular wall,
then shunt the roof right off. Breaking out, they
cheer in bold colours, brandish their golden gloves.

Essentially, Eucalyptus

The Gungurru—*Eucalyptus caesia* Benth—
more beautiful in flower than the Mottlecah,
the Rose of the West. Choose a blossom. It is

a redheaded golliwog; an unruly Ginger Megs;
a fantasia light, yellow bursting
from the tips of a hundred red rods;

a feather duster powdered with pollen;
the nap on a motif on a Persian rug;
a scarlet tassel on the hem of a green robe;

a white-waisted ballerina in a bright tutu;
a coral-coloured sea anemone;
a sea urchin with tube feet but no spines.

These many marvellous things but
essentially this: a eucalyptus flower
with anthers of gold and filaments of fire.

Leaf and Load

The rain is breaking its phials
on the ornamental plum. From
the verandah I choose a leaf,

glistening with wet, and watch
until each vein becomes a rill
running into the midrib-river

and on to the leaf's tip
where the waters gather in a blister
to weight the leaf downwards

by imperceptible degrees. Slipping
from the chlorophyll plane, the rain-
drop hangs from the leaf-tip

as a ball-bearing might hang
from the point of a magnet, held
by the barest contact between

curve and cusp. Like a miniature
transparent balloon tied by a child
to a tap, the drop swells,

bulges with a fragile elasticity,
bowing the leaf with its growing load,
until loosed at last by gravity.

Released, the leaf leaps up,
shudders to an easy equilibrium
in the light, impacting rain.

Spotted Pardalote

Pardon me but
look! A pardalote
in my garden!

See? It is
breaking the brown blisters
on the eucalypt leaves—

probing the sawfly's
sweetpulped larvae.
Now, you were saying?

In the Flame Tree

In the flame tree—

grey and sharp
against the burr of brightness

from branch to
slightly bowing branch

parting the partition
of petals

to taste with tongue
the nectar

far sweeter
than (to a cat) blood

—the wattlebird.

Jacaranda

On the grass by the trunk,
fragments of white shell.

In the crook of two branches,
a thatching of sticks—

and fledglings,
fragile with life.

Scythed bare by the blade of winter,
but comforted by doves,

the jacaranda.

Turtledoves

Beneath the almond tree,
in constant close proximity
to each other, two Indian

turtledoves quick
step nervously on the lawn.
They bob among the broken nut

shells, search for food
fragments fallen from the ripe
white kernels the king parrots

carelessly eat with their hawk
beaks and bean tongues. Some
times nature seems invigorated

by an inadvertent love—
as when the hooligan parrot
helps the immigrant dove.

Colours

i

Colours of sunlight
carpeting the lawn beneath
the autumn almond.

ii

On the grey bark of
the bare almond, green doilies
the lichen crocheted.

Hunting Wren

i

My binoculars—
focused on the kikuyu where
the wren is hunting.

ii

Very vigorous—
the insectivorous wren
hunting on the lawn.

Goshawk

Birds burst from the almond tree.
And looking up I see a goshawk
standing on a branch. Its head
ratchets on its shoulders, yellow eyes
unblinking. It fluffs its feathers,
looks suddenly lighter, bigger—
a bird leavened by blood
in the heart of winter.
It lifts one leg, tucks it
beneath the coverlet of feathers, then
snugs the quill-quilt to the body's bed.
As if a hand had brushed its breast
it is again sharp and sleek. The goshawk,
one-taloned and doveless in the leafless tree.

End of Winter

I marked it only
because of the movement of
a honeyeater—
the first pale blossom to break
from the twiggy almond tree.

Almonds

First a galah, now
a pair of parrots have come
to the almond tree.
Give them up, the unripe nuts,
and accept the birds they bring.

Petal Poem

When the wind flounces the almond tree
petals flurry from the branches
like butterflies caught up in courting.
Exhausted, they spread their wings

on my neighbour's terracotta tiles.
My new neighbour, who felled a red gum
in its frock of white flowers because
it dropped stamens into his gutters.

Garden Violet

i

So unassuming
even the bees have missed it—
the garden violet.

ii

The violet and I—
instinctively we exchange
an Eskimo-kiss.

iii

I lay the violet
on the sink, its stalk dipping
in a water drop.

iv

Again I inhale
and again the small violet
gives itself away.

Plenty

If the lolling weight
of the purple flower-cluster
is not enough, then
add a fidgeting fantail to
the leaning agapanthus stalk.

Perch

Because it is bent,
the stalk of the agapanthus
is a perfect perch
for the fantail, which alights
beside the mauve flower-head.

Struggle

Such a struggle
to disentangle one thread
from the lining
of the old hanging-basket—
yet the finch keeps on yanking!

Ragged

The lining of
the flower-basket hanging
from the rafter
is a little ragged where
the finches have been tugging.

Hatching

The child next-door has
never seen chickens ... I hold
the egg to her ear
to hear the *tup-tep-tapping*,
tell her, 'Soon the shell will break.'

Violets and Chickens

A disturbance
among the lush violet leaves
as the chickens
shoulder between the leaf-stalks
in search of worms and woodlice.

Distraction

So why do I feel
it's wasteful to be watching
in the autumn sun
a swallow preening its tail
on a weathered footbridge rail?

Happy

Happy to be here
on this mild autumn evening
ambling by the marsh—
happy to leave the moaning
mainly to the moaning frogs.

Those Colours

It is hardly beautiful, the bobtail
goanna. Its triangular head
is like a death adder's. Ticks,
cream-coloured, hang at its ears
like enamelled pendants. I squat

for a closer look and it gapes
at me. Those colours: the pale pink
gums, the deep purple tongue and,
most unexpectedly, a yellow flower
blooming in the back of the throat.

Snake in a Box

Who took a stick to you, snake?
Who smashed the mail
of your hexagonal scales?
Flies sip your eyes, suck
your side—burst
like a sausage on a hotplate.
Snake, black-backed and
yellow-bellied, frightening
people to kill you.
Tiger snake, Shere Khan
of the Australian swamps,
why did you leave
your frog and mice
hunting? Just the sight of you
evokes the old enmities—
the bruised head, the wounded
heel—'upon your belly
you shall go'. You shall not
go again, poor snake
in a box in the rubbish bin.

Alarm

i
Premonitions
of my presence unsettle
the heron's poise.

ii
This way, that way—
the anxious white face atop
the heron's neck.

iii
Gawking at me,
the white-faced heron utters
a raucous sound.

iv
Was it some harshness
in my heart set the heron
flapping off, croaking?

Bantam Chickens at Nightfall

Dusk. Outside in their wire-mesh cage
the week-old chickens are chirping. Sharp,
regular, like metal on metal in a machine.

They want to be tucked away in their
cardboard box, with its flaps folded over
for warmth and memories of mother.

They chirp and cheep, urgent and forlorn.
Somehow today I know how they feel—
alone in the world, and night coming on.

Arum Lilies

The arum lilies
in white frocks and flocks across
the paddock—lovely
as yearling lambs, newly shorn,
or angels when Christ was born.

Bushwalking

Should I keep going
deeper into the forest?
Pausing a moment,
I listen and hear once more
the squeals of a ferrel boar.

Desertion

Where the track curves out of sight
between the fire-scarred jarrahs,

shadowy among the shadows but noisy
for the forest litter, kangaroos

are rising and retreating. An awe,
an ache, this glimpse. Proceeding,

I discover where they dozed beneath
the grasstrees. I feel their desertion.

I wonder if I should go on or go back.
Either way, who will give me welcome?

Chuditch

Among all the forgetting, I remember
certain things. Like the night in the car
with my grandfather, how a chuditch
ran onto the road. A spotted native cat.

Humanely, grandfather stopped. He held
it by the tail in the headlights, then
swung it against a tyre. A soft thump.
It is the only chuditch I have ever seen.

Until tonight, when driving home I saw,
I thought, a fox, and swerved to hit it.

Spring

I'm sadly frayed
but the world abounds with spring:
little birds braid
the forest with nests and song,
the sky's inlaid
with pale blue, and bright yellow
flowers invade
the paddocks where the pastures
are green as jade
and lusciously long for lambs
to gambol and lounge and wade.

The Spider Orchids

Already the spider orchids are gone.
The triggerplants are still flowering,
their styles rearing back between
the top two petals like small snakes
ready to strike. Five types of these
four-petalled flowers—from the large
mauve ones like bows for a woman's hair
to the small pink ones with a twist
in the petals like boat propellers.
And everywhere the small, insectivorous
sundews, waving orange handkerchiefs
from their sticky hands. But the orchids
are gone. The white spider orchids
with their wispy petals and tall stems.
Those delicate Australians who by contrast
make the cultivated, immigrant kind
look like gaudy ornaments. I have missed
the splendid spider orchids, their
slender movements in the slightest wind.
I have been too busy for wildflowers
and now, two months into spring, I am
too late. With, to tell the truth
(not that one expects a poem to be true
—who cares if it's true to the facts
so long as it's true to the heart?),
one exception. Beside a granite boulder
I saw a single orchid with one petal
draped across its labellum, like a woman
who hides her face while she weeps.

Butcherbird

Dartling from beneath a stone
a dunnart caught
the quick eye of a hooded bird

The butcherbird quests fur and bone

Dunnart, marsupial mouse,
throat wedged in the fork
of the choking twigs,

the butcherbird's larder and slaughterhouse

Ah life! Such a matter-of-fact kill!
In the bone-smooth tree,
on the whetstone branch

the butcherbird hones its bill

Trap

Winnie-the-Pooh gave him the idea
for a pit trap (not for Heffalumps but)
for rabbits. I suggested a box trap
for bandicoots. His mother thought up
a net trap for rock crabs. To no avail.

So his yearning to Trap Something grew
all holiday long. Then a fairy wren
blundered through the kitchen door,
turning the cottage into a house trap
for birds. The little wren. It had

no chance before his covetous hands,
his adoring eyes. Yielding to his
pleadings, I let him keep it overnight.
When I released it this morning, it
merely hunched on the ground beneath

a woolly bush, its feathers fluffed up,
and grey as the overcast day. Oh, what?
Cold? Hunger? A broken spirit? I sit
on the verandah and read another sad
story by Chekhov. But the bird distracts

me from the book. I go back to find it
as before, eyes closed, tail drooping.
What, what can be done to undo what
I have done? I close my hand over it.
Light as fairy floss, this fairy wren.

On the verandah again, I hold it under
my cardigan for comfort and warmth.
It does not struggle, or even tremble.
I cannot concentrate on Chekhov's art.
I am trapped in life—the wren's, mine.

Lord, pity this sad bird, this sad man.

Beckoning

I know how it will end, of course,
I know of the wilting and fading away,

but that rosebush keeps beckoning me
with its tightpacked whitepetalled buds,

pulling my hand to the picking for
my stoneware vase, my hardglazed heart.

Shock

I was writing about dragons
when a bird mistook glass for air.
The shock of it, that whack
against the window! The bird
fell. The dragons fled.
I stepped out to the verandah
to find a cuckoo gasping
by the wall. A bronze cuckoo,
too hurt to be afraid of my hand.

Lacking a mageword for healing,
a wardword for death,
I dissolved a pinch of sugar
in a teaspoon, dripped
a drop in the back of its throat.
It began to choke, beak agape,
tongue thrusting like a dagger.
Then it grew calm. And I
grew amazed. Astonished at
the wild thing in my palm,
the clarity of glass,
the collision of the two,
the coincidence of my presence.

I placed it back at last
on the verandah in the sun.
Winter sun just warm enough
for a bird in shock to bask in.
And as I kept watch from my desk,
the dragons came back,
came back in a hoard. I invoked
warriors with bow and sword
to divert them away from the bird.

White-Capped Robin

i

So, scarlet robin,
does that dot on your forehead
make you Indian?

ii

Friendly robin
I want a dot on my forehead
too ... *Namestey!*

Resuscitation

i

Winter morning—
a robin resuscitates
the cold campfire.

ii

Pentecostal flame
on a coal in the dead fire—
a robin redbreast!

Fire in the Rain

The wood is wet so the fire is slow.
Then the rain begins again, each drop
a small grenade against the coals.
I squat closer to the flames.
The smoke leans over to hug me.

Nearby, a grasstree stands headless,
like a stove pipe. Its resin-red rim
is glossed with rain. And a robin
alights on it—a yellow robin,
its underbelly brushed with wattle.

The bird looks at me then flies on.
I kick the grasstree over. It breaks
into quoits. I toss them on the fire.
The rain skids down my glasses,
distorting my vision of the world.

Pelicans in Calm Water

i

Rocking, rocking
the hull of the pelican
drifting, drifting.

ii

On an even keel—
a pelican and a dinghy
floating together.

iii

A wave at its bow—
the invisibly propelled
white-hulled pelican.

Fitting

i

A hermit crab—
beachcombing at low tide for
a fitting shell.

ii

A little cramped—
the seashell the hermit crab
tries on for size.

iii

Remarkable—
a hermit crab has restored
life to a shell!

Prawning

Entering the black water
we are surprised by light.
The thread of our net
billows into a luminous lace
and our bodies take a faint hue,
become ghostly in incandescent blue.

A million small creatures celebrate
our every movement.
They burst upon our sight
at the slightest beckoning
and scintillate
for a moment in our wake.

The path we have trawled
is gone without a trace,
but before us the river
is latent with light and grace.

Blowfish

i

Giggling, a young girl
tickles with the tip of her knife
the blowfish's belly.

ii

Gulping in the air
that's killing it, the blowfish
inflates its belly.

iii

'Let me,' the boy begs,
raising his boot high above
the blown-up blowfish.

After a Storm

There was a storm while we slept.
A line of seaweed scallops the sand,
as if the sea had built a levee
against itself. We walk into the wind,

wondering things. What do fish do
when the waves go wild? And what
of those ducks we watched fly out
to the island in the bay last night?

And this seahorse, this seadragon
with its long snout and seaweedy limbs,
what mistake did it make to be caught
in the swell and swilled to the shore?

We collect it for the children, amazed
by the beauty death has not yet erased.

Death

Quiet, little bird,
you are not alone. Rest, lie
lightly in my hand.
Take all the solace you can:
death is just a breath away.

Cricket

An amber cricket
makes her way mechanically
across the concrete.
Eggs must be laid and there is
so much dying to be done.

Desperation

It senses its death,
the small thin caterpillar
fastened to the sill
by a thread to its tail tip.
And yet with the last
of its strength, it lifts its head,
rears up like a snake
at the small spider circling
just out of striking distance.

Redback in Firewood

i

A single movement—
lifting-dropping the firewood
gummed with spider web.

ii

The sound of velcro—
separating the woodblocks
the spider fastened.

iii

Among the ragged
curtains of its exposed nest—
the redback spider.

iv

Redback in firewood—
on its bulbous black body
the colour of flame.

v

After the redback—
reluctant to gather more
firewood in my arms.

Jewel Beetle

Such an elusive
iridescence sheens from your
green-black elytra,
oh jewel beetle! You bask in
rainbows, like a drop of oil.

Wasp

Burying its face
in the white honeymyrtle,
a small wasp, yellow-
and-black banded, bright among
the flurrying, fawn-winged moths

Grasshopper

It imagines, I imagine, the air
turned solid to stop it with a start,
the large grasshopper that just now
whacked into my window. Pressed

unexpectedly to the inexplicable
glass, the creature's underbelly
is marked with two Xs—on the thorax,
between the last two pairs of legs

—two cross-stitches to strengthen
and fasten the muscles. Amazing!
What, I wonder, are the chances
that chance was the seamstress?

Reservoir

A couple of drops
from the sprinkler, and it's full—
the small cavity
in the concrete footpath where
wasps come to drink and make mud.

Drawing Close

Although the distance
between us is not diminished,
through my binoculars
the daisies like small children
draw their faces close to mine.

Street Artist

Using pompom brushes
and a pointillist technique,

a wattle tree has dabbed
a park bench with yellow.

Slaters in Grass

A splicing of shadows and yellows
is the forest of wild oats.

And between the tall trunks
several wood lice, slaters

forage about in their armoured coats
like miniature armadillos.

Raven

The idle raven
turns an eye to the violets
encircling the tree,
the lush violets enfolding
a fearless, henless chicken.

Diversion

Was it me made them
wheel—*Weelah! Weelah!*—away
from the nearest gum
simply to land in the next,
the white-tailed black cockatoos?

After Almonds

i

Oh, is it on fire,
the tree's crown? No, cockatoos
crackling the almonds!

ii

Atop the almond—
black cockatoos hanging on
against a strong wind.

Forest Cockatoos

i

Black cockatoos—
practising crude carpentry
on the pinecones.

ii

After cockatoos—
a litter of wood-shavings
in the pine forest.

Pines

These pines, or the seeds of their parents,
were imported from America.
Planted in Australia, they are perturbed
by memories of the Northern Hemisphere.

See that tree, for instance—the tuft
of dead needles caught in the crook
of branch and trunk. It is the throat-tassel
of a moose—the bell of a big bull.

Look. Many trees have grown beards.
The uppermost branches of some are bare—
all bone and peeling velvet.
They are restless in the rough wind.

Listen. Farther off in the forest,
the clash of antlers!

Palm

The cotton palm. This is it. Do not ask
for more. It is on the Swan River foreshore,
is ten metres tall, has a trunk like the leg
of a pachyderm, has a topknot of green fan-fronds
below which grey leaf-limbs lie overlapping
along the trunk, thick and smooth
as thatching—flattened against the trunk,
head down like dozing bats. But forget
about that. Consider this. Help me create it.

The palm is a great and splendid rooster.
The living leaves are his unruly comb,
the flattened fronds are his neck-feathers.
Imagine that—the green comb, the grey cowl
of the palm-tree-cock. Now see at the base
of the smoothed-down nape, a few feathers
are ruffled, sticking up—as if the rooster
were raising his hackles, being heckled
by the windy crowing of a rival cock.

Green Elephants

The Abyssinian banana trees
in the zoological gardens: surely
they are a herd of elephants
standing on great unbending legs.

And see how here and there a new leaf—
laminae freshly unfolded,
petiole and midrib uplifted—
is a trunk held in salute,

draped ceremonially in emerald cloth.

New Leaf

Spiking from the centre of the older leaves,
extending the line of the trunk
straight up like a green lightning rod
or, later as it loosens, like a rolled newspaper
flaring at the free end: the new banana leaf.
When unfurled, it is unbroken
but lined, as a coupon for tearing.
Newly open, bending slightly
towards the inevitable earth, it is
broad and smooth: a lacquered ceremonial paddle;
an elongated elephant's ear. Then too soon
the wind tugs and teases it,
tears it to tatters until it flutters
shabbily, like a string of streamers at a car yard.

Trimming a Tree

Now, take that tree,
that Norfolk Island pine,
and stand it undiminished
in your imagination.

Next, lop the limbs
a metre from the trunk and
clear the clutter of scaled,
armadillo-tailed leaves.

Note the pattern: the cut
branches radiate in sets
of five or more, like spokes
spiking from a hub.

Now, fell the tree. But
don't let it crash down.
Lower it with ropes (bolt
the pulley to a sure point

in the mind) so as
not to shatter the spokes.
At the outer reach
of each radiation, fix a rim.

See? You have many wheels
on a common axle. It is like
a Roman war machine.
Roll it down the hill.

Let it buck and hurl
against the barbarian ranks.

Not in Truce

Above the black soil of the bulldozed paddock
spiders have spun their threads
on upraised sticks and roots.
In the midst of anarchy, a small affirmation
of design. The webs,
wet with dew and infused with light,
are white pennants raised to proclaim
the mysterious endurance of the powerless.
Or they are bandages of fine gauze,
daubed where limbs have snapped, wrapped
to staunch the flow of beauty from the broken land.

And perhaps it's only little things that will remain
to shore the heart against the broad and brutal ugliness
that looms as the destiny of man. Perhaps
small gestures—the weaving of poems
or the pursuit of a personal integrity
or an unfaltering faith that God is good and
good is no illusion—are all that is left to us.
Like the spiders, we bind the broken roots.
Not in truce, but on trust, we raise
our ragged, regal flags in the winds of a desolate age.

Ford and Trees

Below the confluence of Wooroloo Brook and the Swan
several casuarinas stand in the river, their roots

rising compact and conical above the low water.
A chain downstream, the smooth water widens, drops

as from a ledge, along a row of rounded stones, flows
poppled and scarved with foam over the pebbled shallows.

The casuarina trees are the legs of a draughthorse,
their great hooves tufted, flared with root-hairs.

And the starting stones of the ford are the shares
of a plough, blunt blades of dolerite and granite.

Now see how the horse is drawing the plough
upriver, leaving behind the furrowed water.

See too the kangaroos crossing the long paddock,
their elbowed legs sinking in the loose, white loam.

Nightfall

Sporadically, windfall fruit
stop the deep silence
of nightfall

And then rhythmically—
three, four times—a mute
thud Look!

Between the rows of oranges
through the thighhigh paspalum
a kangaroo

A young doe
scenting out the sweet
lowlimbed pears—

Partripe pears
belling halfyellows
in the beckoning dark

Pygmy Bat

i
Drawing the curtain
to find in one of the folds
a small bat sleeping.

ii
Making a hammock
of itself—the pygmy bat
hanging on the drapes.

iii
Giving new meaning
to 'beady-eyed'—the big-eared
pug-nosed pygmy bat.

iv
The pup of a pug—
that's how you look, pygmy bat,
with that ugly mug!

Straw-necked Ibises

On the grassed river-flats
a flock of ibises—
like elderly Orientals
gathered for a festival.

Bald, whiskered, venerable,
they finick over locusts
and other morsels
with their chopstick bills.

Frogs

i

Chirpy as crickets—
fellowship of little frogs
by the paperbarks.

ii

Only the first week
of winter—what sort of ruckus
in a month, marsh frogs?

iii

Oh stop, you jolly
little frogs—it's unseemly
to be so happy!

iv

As I approach
the paperbarks, one hundred
frogs stop croaking.

Gecko Hunting

i

Glancing out at night—
a gecko's white underbelly
pressed against the pane.

ii

Out of the darkness
it comes, the gecko, to hunt
on my windowsill.

iii

The flustering moth
the gecko just caught—a bit
too big for its mouth.

Good Catcher

i

'It's good you catched him, Dad.'
His voice is remote with reverence
as the gecko sloughs its image in his eye.

How long has it been
since I lived in longing
for lizards?

On the beach I saw
a leatherjack, dry and brittle.
I am like that fish. And yet ...

'Can I keep him? Dad,
why can't I?'

He is too young to know
how some things are crippled by love
if they're not let go.

ii

'Watch how good I catch
this one,' he says.
'Cause she's a bit sick.'

Intently, he shepherds the deformed hen
into a corner, then lunges.

Dazed by a frenzy of wings,
he falls back. He glances at me:
A four year old boy
humiliated by a hen
in his father's presence.

'Whew!' he says, shaking his head.

The chooks are ranged against him
at the other end of the coop.
He eyes them nervously.

'Nearly,' I comfort.

He gathers the eggs quickly.

iii

'I'm a good catcher now,
aren't I, Dad?'
He lets the grasshopper
hop free, then
pounces on it again.
'That's four times,'
he says proudly, holding it
up to me, pincered
between forefinger and thumb.

A bead of black vomit
lubricates its mechanical mouth.
If only he knew
the world is chockfull
of good catchers.

'Son,' I say, 'why
don't you let it go?'

Interval

i

Got to be a first—
a willy wagtail perching
without fidgeting!

ii

Perhaps it's having
a fidgeting intermission—
motionless wagtail.

All-Season Legs

i

Avocet, why
such long legs to wade in such
shallow water?

ii

Avocet, to cope
with seasonal change, you need
adjustable legs!

Between Glances

It is a liquidambar, the tree
I planted two months ago
beside my study. Green and
leafy then, it is almost bare

now. A little twiggy thing.
One red leaf flutters from it
like a child's hand. For a week
it has been waving to me,

wanting my attention, trying
to tell me something unknown
to eucalypts and evergreens.
Something European or Japanese.

Something sad and deciduous.
That brave beautiful leaf,
beckoning the eyes as a flame
beckons the palms. All day

it has warmed me. Exquisite,
that small wind-chafed hand,
its familiar flutter. I glance
down at my work then out

again, only to find it gone.
Gone between glances. If only
I had known that last wave
was a goodbye, a farewell,

I would not have looked away.

My Zebra Finches

It has been a cold night.
Their eyes are closed,
my zebra finches, and their breath
barely comes and goes.

Their bright bills,
so like ill-placed party hats
yesterday, don't seem
ludicrous any more.

I hold them in my hands and
they absorb my warmth
with blind eyes and bills resting
on my knuckles.

After an hour, suddenly,
the hollows of my hands
no longer hold them—
they flick out and flit away.

They are so weak
I catch them easily:
but now they are afraid
and I know they will live.

Grey Butcherbird

I
Executioner

i
It sings sweetly
and yet it wears a black hood—
the butcherbird.

ii
Forget the song—
consider the black hood of
the butcherbird.

II
Threnody and Thanksgiving

i
Hooded butcherbird—
warbling in a ringbarked tree
grace for a dunnart.

ii
Marsupial mouse—
hanging in the butcherbird's
treetop larder house.

III
Coolness

i

Butcherbird drinking—
letting the coolness trickle
down its beak, its throat.

ii

The coolness taking
the taste of blood from its tongue—
drinking butcherbird.

Night Driving, Outback

i

The unending road—
we hurtle deeper into
our tunnel of light.

ii

And then kangaroos
highlighted in our headlights
waiting at high speed.

Cat

A stray ginger cat
just bolted a lump of cheese
my daughter let slip
while lunching awhile ago.
Now it has scrabbled
onto the sag where she sat
in the old deckchair
and is gingerly sniffing,
Eskimo-kissing,
the weathered canvas, testing
tentatively with
whisker and paw the pliant
surface, unsure if
this is where to curl and nap
in the weak midwinter sun.

Shadow

I glance up and—as if
the book I'm reading
were not enough, not
to mention the coffee

I just made, or the sea
sounding behind the dunes,
or the cicadas striking
in the peppermint trees—

as if these were not
enough blessings for
one man at one time—
I glance up and see

the shape of a bird
shaded on a towel
hanging on the hoist.
This life! For a moment,

a moment I happened
to share—a blue towel
with a blue wren drawn
in shadow on its nap!

Tweezers

As with tweezers
a woman pincers precisely
an eyebrow hair—
a honeyeater plucks aphids
from the calyx of a white rose.

Picnic

The picnic table
beside the karri forest—
rufous treecreepers
hop around it now to feast
on the March flies we swatted.

Fan

i

As coquettish as
a courtesan—the wagtail
unfolding her fan.

ii

Red calligraphy—
how it would brighten the slats
of the wagtail's fan!

iii

Haijin Chiyo-ni,
what haiku would you suggest
for the wagtail's fan?

Currawongs

It alighted by the blood blisters
of a plum, my first currawong.

Forgetting the parrots, I lowered
my gun and gawked. It was like

but not a crow—grey, yellow-eyed,
touched white on wings and tail.

It shone in a shaft of sunlight.
A spirit crow, magical, magnificent!

'A squeaker,' the orchardist told me.
'Pests when they were plentiful.'

This morning the currawongs confirm
their common name. A family flock

is rehearsing its varied repertoire
in the house paddock. They squeak

and squawk, harsh and high, as they
fossick or roost or fly. A racket!

Then in a lull one calls, plaintive.
Far off another responds, the notes

identical but transposed. They cry
repeatedly—antiphonal, distinct.

I am sweetly reminded of children
crisscrossing on unoiled swings.

Wool on a Wire

Even a fallen wire fence, it transpires,
has its uses. The top strand—the one
that scribbles through the air from
the tilted star picket to the upright
strainer post—has become a spindle.

Without spinning, it has drawn fibres
from the underbellies of the rams, who
step over it to enter the house paddock.
Baubled with clover burrs, the wool is
wound around the wire in a small skein.

Alighting on the spindle, a thornbill
tugs at the wad, teasing the threads
free. It stuffs its beak with fluff.
Fully bearded, it flies for home with
the resistance of the wind at its face.

Merino Rams

Startled by the dog, the rams
bolt from the fence. But the dog
does not follow its bark, so

the rams stop a short distance
into the paddock and stare back
sheepishly. Such indignity—

sixty studs routed by a single
mutt! Charged with adrenalin
and chagrin, they turn against

one another. Duels break out
throughout the mob. A horned
pair back away from each other,

looking suddenly magnificent—
like the wild rams that once
fought for their flocks in far,

unfenced places. They charge
and clash. A hard, hollow sound.
After the shock, one combatant

crumples, its forelegs folding
first. Elsewhere, more go down
or back off. Then, masculinity

asserted and honour restored,
they settle to their grazing,
undisturbed by the urgencies

and rivalries that will come
with the three thousand ewes
and the rutting in the spring.

Wallabies Grazing

Bush and pasture
brush and posture in sepiagrey
                        and I—
oh the freshandchill, hushandstill dusk!

Look—lesslit
in the pit and pith of my eyes'mind
than the fadeaway pastureslope—
burrshapes
            What?

Not stumps
not stock—not sheep or cattle

I am striding towards them
along the looseloam firebreak
                        Wallabies

Two wallabies
            stockstill, humpshaped
grazing

Thirty yards between us
                  Oh life!
I am so real   I am
bloodandbreathing
rhythmandstriding
How can they miss me?

Startled
they standupandstare
bound to the boundaryfence:
looseshadows in a lostshape landscape

Beneath the Fence

In the loose gravel
beneath the bottom strand of wire
of the boundary fence—
a scraped hollow where kangaroos
cross from the bush to the pasture.

Inebriation

Wanting another
fermented burgundy fruit,
the ringtail possum
overreaches and slips from
the Morton Bay Fig tree.

Possibilities

There must be, I suppose, a measure of thought
and a modicum of volition in a bird's brain.

That western rosella, for instance, perched
on a branch above a patch of dried thistles

and wild oats—see how it turns its head
this way and that, pondering the possibilities:

to fly down or not to fly down? What
tiny cogitations are sparking in its brain?

I await its decision, admiring in the interim
its crimson breast. So bright! Perhaps

if it alights it will set the grass alight.

Everlastings

i

'Ever' is wrong,
paper-petalled daisies, but
'lasting' is right.

ii

Lastingly lovely
despite the overstatement—
the everlastings.

Donkey Orchids

i

Such uncommon
contours and colours, common
donkey orchids!

ii

Belying their name—
the common donkey orchids
braying with beauty.

Arrow Bamboo

i
They pierce the heart
even as they grow—the slender
arrow bamboo shafts.

ii
Alighting mid-stem,
a bird sends a shudder through
an arrow bamboo.

iii
Lacking perfection,
I cut it down—the slightly
bowed arrow bamboo.

iv
As in a quiver,
a bunch of arrow bamboos,
green flights aquiver.

v
Japanese arrow
bamboos stirring ... I think of
samurai passing.

Wind Catcher

Its leaves are catching
the wind, this giant bamboo culm,
but in ancient times
it would have caught it differently,
fixed to mast and sail as a boom.

New Voice

Since being sawn
to shorter lengths and strung up,
the giant bamboo
speaks not in lofty rustlings
but in low chimes and chunkings.

Innovation

Linking Zulu and
Aboriginal know-how,
the hunting egret
has fixed a stabbing spear to
the woomera of its neck!

Offset

That brolga posture
and egret plumage—so grand!
Yet the effect is,
dear spoonbill beside the lake,
quite offset by your namesake!

Heron Standing

i

Without a koan
a Zen heron standing in
contemplation.

ii

A meditation
on stillness—a grey heron
by a swift stream.

iii

Agitating
the bulrushes with stillness—
standing heron.

Pink-and-Grey Galahs

i

A flock of galahs,
pink-and-grey in the white gums,
acting the galah!

ii

No getting round it,
cockies—you're just a gang of
galoots and galahs!

Crossword

i

A flock of finches—
doing a crossword puzzle in
the cyclone wire gate.

ii

Cyclone wire crossword—
in every square and column
the finches put 'finch'.

Cuckoos

Today I heard the pallid cuckoos
summoning each other in the forest
for solace, sex and surrogacy.

For the first time this year
I heard their mournful crescendos
rising above the thin canopies.

The rain has many tireless
tongues. The winter is very grey.
But today the cuckoos called.

In one month it will be spring
and the sun will be bright and warm
like a brood egg in a blue nest.

Bird with Berry

Taking a ripe berry
in the tough tweezers of its beak
and squeezing it until
the flesh bursts out, a currawong
beneath the snottygobble tree.

Black Feather

Is it, this feather
sticking upright in the soft
needle mesh-matting
beneath the pine trees, is it
a lance hurled down in challenge?

Waterlily Haiku

i

In a red gown—
the carp beneath the lily's
green parasol.

ii

A disturbance ...
and then those undulations
in the lily-pads.

iii

Whenever I look
there's never a frog folded
on the lily-pads.

iv

The missing goldfish—
wafting out from the shadows
of the lily leaves.

v

The waterlily—
floating another helipad
for the dragonflies.

Birds Bathing

Despite winter chills—
robins at their ablutions
in a reddish dish
on a stump beside a small
bare tree ringed by daffodils.

Importance

Given that God
did not consider robins
too small to make,
I regard them big enough
for my poems to celebrate.

Removing a Cap

The way a woman might pull a beanie
from her up-gathered hair—first the cap
lifting a little to reveal

the fine hair drawn up in a curve
from the nape of the neck,
then a few strands frizzing out,

freed from the others still crimped
by the wool, until the knitted cap
is right off and her hair springs

loose and light from all constriction,
fans like a nimbus about the head
of a saint, only more sensuous

—that is what it looks like,
the cap lifting from the eucalypt bud,
the filaments, Afro-style, flaring out.

The Muff Bees

My daughter called them 'muff bees',
mistaking them for moths that sting.
But apart from the beauty of her name,
I had thought they were merely ugly,
the March flies, with their blowfly
bodies and cicada wings, their
bulging eyes and long proboscises.
They look like homunculi in gas masks
or bug-eyed children with straws
in their mouths. With those inflexible
trunks, they are tiny winged elephants,
the Dumbos of the insect world.

In the shade of a karri one autumn
I swatted dozens of the suckers
as they came for the blood
that happened to be in my legs. It was
a slaughter. It was a satisfaction.
Inspecting their bodies, I found the pests
guilty of ugliness, their iridescent-
green eyes compounding their crime.

But this afternoon I saw one
hovering in a shaft of sunlight,
its body buoyant, its wings burring,
its proboscis protruding in exact
proportion to its other parts
and angled exquisitely
according to the tilt of the head.
It was like a humming bird.
It was, without a murmur, a muff bee.

Little Tree

That little tree. It is a Japanese
ink painting—wobbly and ill-shapen
yet possessing a strange symmetry.
It is a haiku among the epics
of marri, jarrah and blackbutt.
The bonsai of the Australian bush.
It is something Basho might have seen
on the Narrow Road to the Deep North.

That little tree, *Persoonia longifolia*,
known by the locals as 'snottygobble'.
How unlike the vernacular it is, how
unsnotty, how very eye-gobbling! A mop
of greenery among the grey eucalypts.
Those long, thin leaves. Even the bark
is beautiful—many-layered, thick
and spongy, like a ream of rice paper.

So many layers! Every limb is plump
with bark, as if wrapped in puff pastry.
Gawky and gangly, it is nonetheless
quite glorious, that little tree.

Pine and Poem

Unlike other trees, the Norfolk Island pine
neither gives up and droops over nor disperses
into branches. No weeping, no compromise.

It surges straight up. Even its laterals
support the single perpendicular.
Each ring of branches is a set of guys

anchored to the sky to keep the centre post
poised. Diminishing in diameter,
the spoked strata shape a tent

as a farthingale shapes a dress.
The green frame, tall, conical, waiting
to be covered. Trim the sky for a canvas.

Peg it down. Don't let it flap loose
from your imagination. Gales are gathering.
Strong winds are coming. Stake out

your tent. Enter in. Enter in to the calm.

Gladdened by Ibises

As unexpected as the first sighting,
this remembrance of those ibises.
By-passing my retina, they enter
my brain, shimmer like mirages
in the blackness of my skull.
A pair of sacred ibises, white-
bodied, black-necked and -tailed.
Standing knee-deep in the kikuyu
on the river bank in the park,
they preen themselves awkwardly
with their long curved beaks.
Sicklebirds. One turns its bill sideways
to scissor its breast feathers,
while the other bends its neck
to probe the plumage between its legs.
Inexplicably, I see them as I saw them.

And it occurs to me that those birds
are somewhere out there still,
still being ibises, still doing
ibisy things. Impervious to me,
they occupy the same time as me
but move in a different space.
Where, I wonder? What swamp, creek
or weir? Perhaps they never left
the park. Or have returned. Yes.
Surely they are in the park now
with someone about to see them!
Someone I don't know. A woman,
perhaps. A middle-aged woman who,
being a little chunky and melancholy,
is out walking to lift the weight
from her hips, her heart.

Glancing up she sees them, the same
ibises I saw, the very pair I see
in the virtual reality of my head!
And she thinks, *Oh, a white bird*
with a black bustle! Two of them.
And she stands for a moment, simply
gladdened by ibises. The nearest one
twists its liquorice-stick neck
to settle a feather on its shoulder.
Then suddenly alarmed, it croaks
and takes to the clear cold air,
its companion following close.
And she watches them go, this woman
whose life my life has never touched,
watches those sacred ibises wing
along the glossy water and round

the river bend. And when at last
she moves on she hardly feels
any weight at all. She could almost
skip, skip like her granddaughter,
as she walks with those white birds
spreading their wings in her mind.

Birds in Mind

i

Sacred kingfisher—
into the world onto the branch
courtesy the King.

ii

Wren and the art
of bird-making—dear Lord, such
blue in the bush!

iii

Statuesque heron—
unmoved as humans debate
the Sculptor question.

iv

Goodness, that ibis
signals the presence of birds
in the mind of God!